while you are healing

parm k.c.

@byparmkc

ISBN: 979-8-3604740-5-0

for the ones who feel broken.

i hope you find light and empathy
among these pages.
i hope my words will
soothe your heart
while you are healing.

contents

this
doesn't

feel
like

love

while you are healing

that was the last time
i let someone hurt me,
i tell myself
as i fall for another wrong one.

9

loving you
is like making shapes out of clouds.
if i try hard enough,
i can imagine anything i want.
i can create what i wish to see
using simply my imagination.
it works with the clouds.
it works with you.

dear love:
i'm sorry so many ugly things
are impersonating you.

i wonder often
if i am good enough for you,
if i am beautiful enough for you,
if i am strong enough for you.
i wonder often
if i am enough for you.
i don't wonder often enough
if you are enough for me.

the slow death
of being with you.
of pieces of me dying,
of my spark gradually fading,
of feeling myself
vanish.

☐

i ask you if you love me,
and you hesitate.
the pause is brief but loaded.
i know what it means.
i know what lies in that empty space.
i almost don't need you
to say anything else,
but you do.
it's a shaky and uncertain *yes.*
i welcome it all the same.
i let out a sigh of relief,
content that despite being unable to feel the
yes,
i hear it.
content that i can hide from that pause
a little longer.

a person is so much more
than a promise.
make sure you love the person,
not their promises.
make sure you see
the difference between the two.

i would like to love someone
in a way that doesn't feel
quite so thankless.

you tell me i am beautiful,
and i cringe.
not because i don't believe you,
but because i know beautiful
is all you think i am.

i know you see me
without really seeing me.
you see a face and a body.
you see eyes and lips.
skin and hair.
you see everything that is part of me,
but none of what is genuinely me.
you see what you can show others -
what you can hold up as a trophy.
what you can call your own.
but you do not see me.

you tell me i am beautiful,
and i cringe.
but i smile and i accept it.
because i'd rather you see
what you think is me
than not see me at all.

how to extend pain:
resist the lesson.
assume you know better than fate.

be careful.
someone who is confused
about what they want
can cause you to become confused
about what you're worth.

don't trust anyone's word
more than you trust your own instinct.

-intuition

we know deep down when someone says
i love you,
but doesn't mean it.
we stay anyway
because we want to hear the words.
the words seem like enough -
we make them be enough.
it's not about feeling love.
or knowing love.
or being in love.
it's about the words.
if we are creative enough,
desperate enough,
lonely enough,
we can mold the words
into something they are not.
twist them.
shape them.
form them into something
that emulates the real thing
enough for us to be satisfied.
we let the words fill in
where the person falls short.
and then sometimes,
whether you can feel the love or not,
i love you
is just nice to hear.

oh how i wish i could see myself
as i am.
not as he treats me,
but as i am.

you speak to me in cruelty,
and it is not a dialect i understand.
i was taught to be soft.
i was taught never to raise my voice.
so yours drowns mine out -
and in the process,
i drown too.

i went into the woods last night,
found the ravine,
dipped my toes in the water.
prayed to the night -
let him love me.
let me be the one.
submerged myself fully
knowing good and well that
my prayer would not be heard
and that if he cannot embrace me
at least nature and her touch
will.

parm k.c.

i think i am more in love
with what we could be
in another incarnation -
in another world -
than what we are
here and now.
it's the fantasy tying me to you.

i imagine a world
where you think i'm enough,
and that's enough to keep me with you.

parm k.c.

begging for love
and being in love
are not the same.

27

we say hurt people hurt people.
but i don't want to make excuses
for the ones who hurt me.
healed people
stay away from hurtful people.

there are too many people
pretending to love,
and too many people
desperate for anything
that resembles love.
somehow they keep
finding each other.

he hurts you,
and you try harder.

-insanity

i see those lovers -
the ones i wish we could be.
the snuggle up at dinner lovers.
the hand in hand,
matching outfits lovers.
the going in the same direction lovers.
there is no me without you lovers.
i want to be them but
we are something else entirely.
we are the destined to fail lovers.
wear my anger like a cloak and
call it love lovers.
we are throwing pots and pans
at two a.m. lovers.
angst and contempt but still together lovers.
break each other so thoroughly
that we're left unrecognizable lovers.

i keep wanting to be chosen.
as though i need others
to tell me i'm worth something
before i'll believe it myself.

i am studying you
like art on the wall
and wondering who
hung you there because
even though there is nothing
original about you,
i've convinced myself you
are unlike anyone
i've met before.

i don't know if my love for you
is more ocean or puddle.
all i know is that
it's water in the way
you find a way to drink it up,
then turn around
leaving me parched.

can someone please tell me
how to move through this destruction
without being irreversibly destroyed?

it should not be this hard
to love someone.
it should not be this hard
to be loved.
i think we're doing this wrong.

i pick a star in the sky.
a random star -
and decide
this is the one i'll wish on.
there is no rhyme or reason
but i want to feel
like something is mine.
it doesn't matter to me
that others might be wishing on it too.
i cannot see them -
i see nothing more than the star.
i pretend the star is mine
and it will grant all my wishes.

i see you like this star.
a reflection of all my hope -
not really mine
but bright enough
that i can pretend you are.

i don't want to go back
to the girl i was before you.
she was the one who let you in.
she got me into this mess.

it's like i am letting you
skin me alive.
peel away my flesh
layer by layer and
instead of stopping you,
i am letting it bleed -
letting you continue.
letting fresh air
kiss raw wounds
because you tell me this
makes you feel alive.
and not only do i want to
feel alive too,
but i can't seem to bear to
be alive without you.

i rushed myself in
to love with you,
and waited patiently
for you to reciprocate.
i told myself
you'd get there eventually.
my patience is selective.

☐

i paint my love onto others,
and then revel in their charm -
believing they are something special
and something more than i deserve.
i overlook the fact that it is
my love
my color
my art
i covered them in
that is making them seem so beautiful.

you are the app
i keep opening,
then closing,
then opening.
i hope to find something
different there each time
but never do.

love is crazy.
sometimes it tells you
to lose yourself
to gain someone else.
☐

your pain is not the disease -
your pain is a symptom
of loving the wrong one.

i want to love in a way
that does not leave me damaged.
i've only ever known the kind
that does.

i can't keep loving people
who don't love me
and crying at the injustice of it.
i don't have enough tears for this.

it shouldn't hurt this much.
i tell myself,
as i continue to love you anyway.

pour me
another bottle of wine,
let me lap it up.
let it go straight to my head -
let it leave me
dizzy.
i need to feel intoxicated
by something other than you.

i keep slicing away
at myself.
hoping i will never
overshadow you -
hoping this will
satisfy you.
i become
less,
and less,
and less.
am i slight enough now?
it seems i've made myself so small
you can't even see me.

how much love
do i have to give
before i realize
i deserve some too?

please take me off
your pottery wheel.
i am tired of being
molded by you.

can you name one reason
you love me -
other than that i love you?

if i'm going to be angry at you
for not loving me,
for not appreciating me,
for not cherishing me -
then i should be angry at me too.

-fair

i don't know why i expect you
to love me forever
when you barely love me now.

you are not gentle with me,
you are not kind to me,
you are not loving towards me.
but i don't care.
you are with me
and i take that as enough.

i am ripping off the bandage,
you say.
as though that doesn't still tear my skin.
as though hurting me quickly
doesn't hurt me.

if you want to leave,
please leave.
but take all of you with you.
and i do mean all of you -
take your memories and your clothes.
take your promises and your books.
take the future we mapped out
and the photographs on the walls.
i don't want to come upon anything
and feel myself break again.
take it all,
leave nothing.
i don't want scraps of you -
i want every last bit,
or nothing.

look at how we seem
when i write about us.
somehow,
i manage to make the poison poetic.
on pages we are not so bad.
in reality,
we are toxic.

parm k.c.

you could not love
someone like me.
but you were happy to use
someone like me.
you taught me that not everyone has
good intentions.

you have been planting seeds where this is no hope for anything to grow, and then feeling despair over the lack of fruit. you have been planting seeds where the soil is rotten and nutrients are scarce. you have been planting seeds where there is no sun. you have been planting seeds where there is no rain. you have been planting seeds in people who would not share the fruit with you even if it, by some miracle, grew.

you can see it coming
from a mile away
and still,
heartbreak collides into you.
the impact will destroy you.
i'm sorry you couldn't seem to
step out of the way.

while you are healing

parm k.c.

nights

that

are

too

LONG

while you are healing

it's hard to lift myself out of bed.
it's hard to let my feet touch the ground
and believe i can make it through the day -
another day,
one more day.
just make it through today,
and then do it again tomorrow.

can someone please show me
another way around the tears
and the nights that don't seem to end?
i wish not to move through this -
this is not the road i'd like to travel.
turn me around,
find me an exit ramp.
let me bypass the breaking
that i know is imminent.
i'd like to take the road that allows me
to close my eyes for a moment,
open them,
and be over you.

let this day be over.
let me crawl into bed
the way i used to crawl into you.
cradle myself,
shut my eyes,
and shut out the world.
let me quiet the hum in my head -
the one that started when you left.
let this day be over
so i don't have to pretend
to be happy,
to be sane,
to be healing.
let this day be over
so i can pull the covers
and the night over me,
let them envelope me and be my comfort.
in the dark i can pretend you're still here.
in the dark i can pretend i feel light.

tell the sun i cannot meet her today.
tell her i know she is waiting -
i know she is burning
just for me.
tell the moon i'll be arriving early
this evening.
that i will tuck myself
into her glow before she is likely
ready for me.
tell every noise in the night
to keep it down -
hush, please.
i have been snapped in two,
(though it feels more like four)
and i need my rest.

over time pain becomes a companion.
it fills the space where he used to live.
it becomes the next *something*
that seems preferable to being alone.

when it hurts too much,
i will ask nothing more of myself
than to take the next breath.

let me write you down
before i forget you,
before you slip through
the cracks of my mind.
let me write you down.
if i can't touch you -
if i can't have you beside me -
let me have you on paper
and let me feel you
from here on out
by forever turning pages.

i have felt it -
the place you are now.
i have lived there and i have
almost died there.
your heart hurts,
as well as every bone
inside your body.
from the top of your head
to the tips of your toes,
it hurts.
you're weary.
he's gone,
and the silence is deafening.
i've been there
and i know.

parm k.c.

grief does not care
how many days or nights
you've counted since he left.
it can stay by your side
longer than he ever could.

i have no solid proof
you were ever really beside me.
your things are gone,
your half of the closet is empty,
there is only one toothbrush
on the countertop now.
somehow i feel your
gone
more than i ever felt your
here.

i thought i would die
when i lost you.
i didn't die,
but this pain
cannot possibly be
how living should feel.

you live in a cloud
that lives in my mind.
it feels like it never
stops raining.

there is no map
for this kind of lost.
there's no clear way out
when you've vanished in someone
who has left you.
this feeling is displacement.

there are
over 7,100 languages.
i would have accepted *i love you*
in any one of them.

i had my feet planted
so firmly in pain's soil
that i couldn't see
i was planting more pain.
watering it with tears.
helping it grow.
i haven't had much luck with gardening
but i've never watched anything
bloom like this.

when people ask me
what happened between us -
why we're no longer together -
i don't know what to tell them.
i don't know how to tell them you broke me.
or that i let myself be broken.
i don't know how to describe
a car crash in human form.
i don't know how to reduce to words
the way we fractured
and cracked along each backbone.
creating a chasm too small for love,
but plenty big enough for pain.
i have no idea how to tell them
that we ruptured each other.
that we entered one another whole
and exited each other torn apart.
i don't know how to tell them any of this,
so i don't.
instead i say,
we just didn't work out.

how did your love
dissolve so quickly?
how did we have such
different definitions
of the word *forever?*

if i could,
i would throw myself
at the hands on the clock.
beg them not to move.
hold them down.
stop them from pushing forward.
i don't want time to march on.
it is pulling me so far from you.

i am so tired.
but not in the way
that can be cured with rest.
i am tired in the way one is tired
when they gave too much
of themselves away.
and loved one too many people
who did not love them back,
and now they are purely
depleted.

i was taught to look both ways
before stepping into the street.
but no one told me to look both ways
before stepping into a person.
i wasn't taught that if i'm not careful -
that if i don't look left and right,
that if i only look ahead
at where i hope to go,
without looking at what might be coming -
what might be on the verge
of barrelling into me -
what might take my legs
out from under me -
that i could break.
i could shatter and find my limbs
and my heart
and my life
scattered.
i wish someone had told me.

i grew weak
from having to audition for your love.
of having to put on a costume and a mask,
read from the script you handed me,
be what you needed,
and nothing else.
i grew tired of wondering
what you would do if i improvised.
would you keep me in the role?
would i lose the part?
ours was a play written solely by you.
not once did i get a chance
to sit in the director's chair.

i could burn down this house -
this street -
this town -
and still,
it would not expel
these memories of you.
you are too deeply entrenched
and i am too deeply surrounded.

i knew you loved someone else
and i loved you anyway.
maybe i don't deserve this pain,
but i sure did see it coming.

please don't tell me
that you never meant to hurt me.
you hurt me,
and this is all that matters.

i want to be autumn.
i want it all
to fall off my branches.
i want to hibernate for a while,
and then start fresh.

i am certain the sun
doesn't feel like waking every day,
but she does so anyway.
i try so hard to be like her
but i can't seem to find a way.

i found her.
it wasn't that hard.
type in a first name,
an occupation -
everything is at your fingertips these days.
i tried to make myself
weep a little less by saying things like
she's not that pretty.
since when do you like freckles?
blue eyes - how original.
i'm sorry to say
i forgot the girl code
when i came for her
instead of coming for you.
i'm sorry to say
it touched a wound to see
you loving her
instead of loving me.

the hardest part is wondering
if the reasons you don't love me
are the same reasons i don't love me.

-insecure

i think about the books i love
and how when i read them
for the first time,
i kept reading
despite knowing they would end.
i still wanted to experience them.
i knew i'd be sad when they ended
but i'd think to myself,
that is a problem for a me
that doesn't exist today.
i think about how when i first
flipped through the pages
i would devour them
with increasing intensity
the closer i got to the end.
despite knowing that i was
rushing myself toward heartache.
despite knowing that i was
rushing myself into sadness.
i think about the way i pushed through
anyway.
and i am reminded of the way i loved you.

i don't know if you loved me,
and i never did.
i didn't need to know.
or rather -
i didn't want to know.
because i learned a long time ago
not to ask questions that have answers
i may not like.
if you don't ask the question,
then you won't hear the *no*.
if you don't hear the *no*,
you can keep pretending it's a *yes*.

it felt like breath itself
had been taken from me
the night you said goodbye.
i drove home hoping
i could keep inhaling
and exhaling
long enough to get there.
the more i tried,
the less i could.
i recall thinking to myself -
i have nothing anymore.
not even air.

maybe if i stand
on the tips of my toes
and stretch up my arms
as far as they will go,
i can pull some stars
down from the sky.
i just really need some light.

after you,
i grew to hate my wristwatch.
i grew to hate my alarm clock.
i grew to hate anything that measured time.
it was like they were all taunting me,
reminding me that moments
were moving forward
and i wasn't.
every tick,
every second,
every red glowing number
was yet another sign
that time was taking me
further and further away from you
and closer and closer to a reality
where you don't come back.

when i say i'm doing okay,
i don't mean i'm doing okay.
i mean i'm not feeling
as broken as i was yesterday.

-progress

i find myself wondering
how many people have fallen in love
since we fell out.
i wish them a better outcome than ours.
a little less pain,
some more hope.
i cross my fingers for them,
and say a silent prayer
like i once did for us.
i can't stand the thought
of others hurting like this.

i guess i was fine
with you not really loving me
because i didn't really love me.
for once,
we were on the same page.

you said *i love you*
and i heard
i'll love you forever.
so now i'm feeling let down
and realizing it wasn't what you said
that let me down.
it was what i wanted you to say,
and the meaning i attached to it
all on my own.

it was nothing light and airy.
it felt full of iron,
and it was pulling me down.
it was nothing i could hold onto -
nothing i could sink my teeth into
and feel was mine.
it was knives in my mind,
day in and day out.
i think i knew it wasn't love.

i pray that the next girl who loves you
is a little bit stronger than me.
i pray she doesn't break as easily.
i pray her grip on herself is firmer
than mine was.
i pray she uses her voice
and i pray you actually hear her.
i pray she doesn't lose herself in you
and i pray she doesn't feel as lost
if she loses you.
i pray for more for her -
i don't wish this on anyone.

it is painstaking -
the process of removing myself
from your belly.
it is prying mouths open,
and severing hope.
it is gasping for air,
and all my energy
not to be swallowed again.
to get myself out.
to barely get out.
only to find i am nothing like the girl i was
when i went in.

i am in awe of my own imagination.
the way i can write stories onto people.
the way i wrote stories onto you.
the way i created a character out of you -
one who looked like you,
sounded like you,
laughed like you,
but was not you.
i wrote you into a love story.
i made you the prince and
me the heroine.
i wrote a happy ending
and it all seemed so real.
but you were not the prince,
i was not the heroine.
i am just that imaginative.

the ones who are happy to touch you
but never truly hold you
do not love you.

i am trying to understand
how you love old cities
enough to hop on planes.
endure 15-hour flights
to see buildings in ruins -
undone and like ghosts
of what they once were,
in shambles from decades
and generations of trauma.
but wanted nothing but distance
from me when you learned that
i have a past and history too.

everyone keeps telling me
let it go.
let it go where?
there is nowhere on earth
or any other planet
that could fit all of this hurt.

there are places i can't go anymore -
you live in them.
you are embedded into their foundation,
and your voice
seems to play through their speakers.
our memories are trapped
on menus
in trees
on park benches.
i don't go there anymore.
i don't go anywhere i might see you
if i'm not really going to see you.

it's okay if you're not at
the healing part yet.
or the growing part,
or the blooming part
of this heartbreak thing.
if you're in the thick of the pain,
if you're so deep in rock bottom,
you are not alone.

don't be afraid to cry them out.
eventually both the tears
and the missing them
will stop.

i remember the night
i was lying beside you
and suddenly,
it dawned on me
how lonely i felt.
i wanted to wake you up and tell you
so that i could feel less alone
in my loneliness.
because i knew deep down,
you felt it too.
i thought if we could feel it together,
then at least that would be
one thing we shared.

they tell you that finding love
feels like falling.
but no one tells you that losing love
feels like crashing.
like impact and collision
and seeing your heart scattered.
wondering how bits of it
landed all the way over there.
no one tells you that it is
shrapnel and glass everywhere.
that you now have to be
careful where you step
because if you're not,
you might find yourself
bleeding all over again.
and that you will be endlessly
pulling shards of the one who left you
out of your mind.

when dark falls
i get to take off the mask
and the pressure
and be me.
i think the moon knows me
better than anyone.

i tell myself that
everyone who feels
incredibly strong,
once felt
incredibly broken.
and often,
this is how i face the days.

why are the ones
who are the hardest to forget
the ones who forget us so easily?

you taught me
people can still drown
in shallow waters.

with you,
it didn't feel quite like falling in love.
there was no soaring through the sky.
it was weights on my chest
so heavy
i thought they might come out my back.
with you,
it didn't feel quite like falling in love.
it felt like being held down.

i am the youngest of three
and the easiest to please.
i am used to hand-me-downs -
used to taking things that
might not fit
and finding a way
to make them do so regardless.
i am used to squeezing myself in
to spaces and things where
i may not belong
and making no fuss about it.
you were no different than
a winter coat i didn't have to buy -
someone else might have
fit me better
but i made do with you.

the pure confusion
of loving someone who hurt you.
of wanting them to return to you,
but feeling relief when they don't.

i placed you on a throne
fifty feet above me.
left you there,
looked up,
grovelled at its base.
no wonder i could never
reach you.

i don't know if i loved you,
or if i loved the way it felt to tell others
i was in love.
so that i could convince the world
i deserved love.
so that i could convince myself
i deserved love.

ever since i was a child
i have loved driving around
to look at beautiful houses.
i create a narrative for them -
imagine who lives there,
the life they lead,
who they love.
i tell myself i know their history
and know their bones.
i tell myself
by looking at the outside
that maybe i could live there -
maybe this would be a lovely place
for me to reside.
this is what i did with you too.

i hardly ever heard *i love you*
escape from your tongue.
but those words would tumble
so easily from mine.
so i convinced myself
we just spoke different languages.

parm k.c.

i was giving love,
and receiving none.

i am still convinced
we could have worked.
if only you had been
none of the things you were,
and everything i wished you were.

you know they didn't love you,
but you still hope they miss you.

-*optimist*

your memory is a bruise
i keep pressing on.
i know it's going to hurt,
but i just need to check.

there are some metals
that explode instantly
when exposed to water.
it's a phenomenon of science
i don't fully grasp,
nor can i explain it.
but i lived it.
i don't know
which of us was the metal,
and which of us was the water.
but it's what happened to us.
it's what happened to me.

i remember our trip to the beach.
it was my first time seeing the ocean
and i didn't know how to swim.
you knew i was terrified,
and you laughed
when you threw me in.
i held back tears and asked you
why you did that.
you said -
i'm teaching you how to survive.
i'm teaching you how to swim.

i think about this a lot.
how you often threw me
into the deep end of things.
how, without my permission,
you taught me how to survive.
you taught me how to swim.

every time someone leaves
i berate myself as though
i chased them away.
i know i didn't.
i know i don't have that power.
but i cannot help but place the blame
squarely on my own shoulders.
this load is too much
and i'm buckling under the weight of it.

i would like to forget you.
but more than this,
i would like to forget who i was
when i was with you.

i see waves crashing into sand
and it makes me think of you.
the way you crashed into me -
turning me soft.
changing my structure.
leaving me weaker,
leaving me heavier,
then changing direction.
returning to your home
utterly unfazed.

i have realized
i am not more alone
without you
than i was
with you.
after all,
i was the only one
in that relationship
in love.

i thought it was romantic
how it was always dark
when i was with you.
i persuaded myself we were
dancing under a night sky.
i didn't know it was so dark
because you had taken
all the light from me.

i don't need you to come back -
in fact i hope you stay gone.
but what i do need is for
me to forget you soon.

you were the cosmic event
that split my being in two.
the big bang
that sent me in two directions.
there was the me before you,
and the me after you.

i need to stop losing myself in people -
i'm rarely provided an exit path.
i do not have a compass.
i wander in them far too long
and cannot steer my way back out.

i was not your home.
i was simply a safe place -
a soft space -
for you to land
while you passed through.
the trouble is,
i made you my home.
i made you my dwelling.
i put down roots and now
they rip and pull from the ground
as you turn to leave.
it kills me.
it's almost like you're
tearing them out of me.
it's almost like you're
tearing love out of me.

it's more than i can endure -
the way night feels relentless
and day feels bleak.
when they leave and you feel lonely,
you realize you should have
gotten to know yourself
a little bit better so this wouldn't happen.
so i will try now.
i will fill the emptiness with myself
so that the next time someone leaves
(i hope they don't, but they might)
i won't feel so empty.
i won't feel so desolate.
i won't feel like i've lost everything.

i can't hold onto you any longer.
your memories must weigh
a thousand pounds.
my arms are too tired.
from holding them,
and the grief,
and the loss,
and the anger at myself.
so i'm going to put it all down,
(yes, all of it)
rest a bit,
and keep going
without you.

their love
is not a substitute
for your love.
give to yourself
whether or not they stay.

i don't know how to relate to the word
healing.
it feels awkward in my mouth -
like my tongue can't fully form around it.
it implies to me a finality
to the business of losing someone.
i'm reluctant to land there -
at that place that is a nail in the coffin
of the grief that has kept me company
for so long.
even if it's better than where i was before,
it's frightening.
it's a form of me i fear i can't live up to.
i might be able to step into her shoes for
a day,
a week,
a month.
but how long can i fool people?
how long can i fool myself?
and when i heal,
will i know i'm healed?
when i heal,
will the ones who hurt me
know i'm healed?

if you stay too long
around people who treat you
like you are not worthy of love,
you will start to believe
you are not worthy of love.

-you are a product of your environment

it was all too easy for me
to toss me aside
when i found you.
we do that sometimes -
abandon our friends
for the love interest.
we find out later
that it was our friends
we should have chosen
and not them.
so now i apologize to her -
to the friend in me i tossed aside.
i tell her i am sorry.
and that something shiny and new
caught my eye.
but the shiny thing was also sharp -
it cut me deeply.
i see now i should not have
picked it up in the first place.
i should not have set her down -
i should not have set me down
for someone else who would
toss me aside too.

it's not the pain that breaks you -
it's your mistaken belief
that it won't ever subside.

i turned myself inside out
to remove you from me.
there was so much of you
left in so much of me,
and i didn't want to leave
even the smallest trace behind.
i felt like i needed to start over.
like i would need a new body,
new skin,
a new existence
to have a me untouched by you.
i needed a me untouched by you.

you look so happy with her -
it's not a smile i recognize.
it's not a smile i ever inspired.
she looks so happy with you -
it's not a smile i recognize.
it's not a smile i ever wore.
maybe you and her are more right
than you and i ever could have been.

parm k.c.

please don't rush me towards healing.
it is weighed down under too much
and i need time,
rest,
and strength
to dig my way out.
i need to lift everything off -
every past love,
every version of me i no longer know,
every goodbye.
these things are so full
and i need to work up my strength
to push them away.
i need time.

i learned this the hard way:
trusting someone
doesn't mean they are
worth your trust.

every time i try to speak about you,
i choke.
the words burn my throat
and bubble on my tongue
and i can't get them out.
it's like your memory
is as toxic as you were.

i have so many questions
like,
why didn't you love me?
why did you have to go?
but most importantly,
where do i look
to find myself now?

i did everything wrong with you.
i handed over too much of me.
i never said *no*
when i wanted to.
i always said *yes*
even when it felt like venom
leaving my lips.
i could see myself
getting smaller,
and smaller,
and smaller.
did nothing to stop it.
watched myself
become someone else -
someone sheepish,
quiet,
someone i didn't recognize.
i did everything wrong with you
and now i am going to try
to make things right
with me.

no one who makes you
feel that small
could possibly be
the one for you.

i didn't feel secure with you.
i didn't know i was supposed to.
this is the danger of loving
without first being taught
what love should feel like.

i don't know how to move on.
but i know i need to move on,
and this is the first step.

the healing i do
is the bridge between
the me i used to be
and the me i am becoming.
i don't know what's on the other side
and i am terrified.
but i do know i need to cross.
what's there
has to be better
than what's here.

i'm not afraid to be alone,
i'm afraid to feel alone.
this is why i need to let you go.

i didn't even care
that you did not love me back.
i tried to love enough for the both of us.
i even had enough,
or so i thought.
but you did nothing but take.
so eventually even that ran out.
thank God it did because it wasn't until
i was drained of everything
that i acknowledged -
i deserve something too.

no matter how much it hurts today,
i know i will meet my true self
at the end of this.

when you left i cried for you.
but i didn't just cry for you -
i also cried for the me
i think i might have been
had i never encountered you.
had i never lived through you.
had i never had to recover from you.
i cried for her naivety and her innocence
and the way she believed
in so many impossible things.
so when you left,
i found myself drowning
in twice the tears.

i don't know if it is love
i am looking for,
or just a place
that feels like home.

i think i saw you
not as someone to love,
but as someone to live in.
i burrowed deep
and latched on.
i didn't consider if i belonged there
or not.
so when i eventually looked around
and took stock of where i was,
and how cold and un-home like it was,
i thought to myself -
how the hell did i get here?

there are parks and theaters and restaurants
that have your name on them.
your memory is etched into their walls.
these are spaces that know you're gone.
i cannot visit them without them asking me
what happened?
or without them asking where you went -
without them asking why i'm alone.

there are songs that wonder
why i'm listening to them without you.
there are photo albums that wonder
where the boy in the pictures went
and why the girl from the pictures
looks so sad.

i cannot answer their questions.
i cannot take the hurt.
it's like you live there,
in all these places,
without truly being there.

so to avoid the questions
(and to avoid you)
i don't go to those places anymore.
i don't listen to the songs.
i don't open the photo albums.
you left,
and now i think it's best that i leave too.

the next time
i come upon love,
i hope not to plummet into it.
i hope not to jump in headfirst.
instead,
i will slowly trace my finger
along its edge.
i will dip my toe in gently.
test the waters,
make sure i see what's down there,
before i let myself fall.

it's not that i'm scared
to love again -
i'm scared to love
someone like him again.

of course i can't stop writing.
of course the poems won't stop flowing.
i was so silent with you.
you kept me so silent,
the words marinated inside of me.
they sat and they festered.
they steeped and they multiplied.
now you're gone
and there is nobody
holding a hand over my mouth,
so the words are spilling out.
and yes, they are hot
from living inside of me -
they are potent and boiling.
they have been burning a hole through me.
they do not flatter you.
they are my truth.

i am so relieved
we didn't get the matching tattoos.
i would have been stuck with you
on my skin
and on my heart,
instead of just on my heart.

maybe it matters less
where you end up,
and more
where you choose not to stay.
maybe moving on
is less about reaching a specific place,
and more about finding a way
to leave the place that hurts.

i grew tired of falling
and hoping he would catch me.
i grew tired of expecting arms,
but hitting the ground instead.

it's not really you who i miss.
i miss who i convinced myself you were
before i truly saw you.
though you two look the same,
you are completely different people.

i am trying to remember how it felt
to meet you for the first time.
how it felt to see your face
and not know how cruel you could be.
to appreciate your laugh
and not hear you laughing at my pain.
i am trying to remember what it felt like
to think of you and feel hope.
to think of you and feel something
other than anguish.
to think of you
and still think of me
positively.
sometimes i wish i could go back.
not so i can meet you again,
but so i can meet the me i used to be.
so i can warn her.

i didn't care that it wasn't love.
i only cared that at times,
it felt like love.

you were like summer.
in the dead cold of winter,
it seems so appealing.
when it first emerges,
it warms your chilled bones.
but by the end of it,
the heat is too much to bear.
it is no longer warm -
it burns.
and you find yourself
ready for fall.

there was what i deserved,
and what i accepted.
and somewhere in the canyon
between the two
was you.

each hurt a lesson.
each loss a poem.
all this wisdom
and so many pages
and somewhere in it all,
finding my way to me.
☐

i think if i can
keep taking breaths,
and letting them go -
one after another,
then i can begin
to let you go too.

healing comes in parts.
the first part is the breaking.

i can call your leaving a void,
or i can call your leaving
the catalyst for my birth.

if i keep looking back,
i won't be able to move forward.
so in the name of moving forward,
i simply need to let you go.

you hold onto this pain
as tightly as you once held him.
it is the last connection you two have.
you fear if you let it go,
you let him go.
it's time to release them both.

i was never yours.
you were never mine.
we were passing through each other -
a layover,
a stop on the way to other destinations.
cities we would not have otherwise visited.
and certainly not places either of us
would ever have chosen to live in.

the way some people treat you
feels like a slow death.
the way they belittle you,
and shrink you,
and turn you into a shell of yourself.
the way some people treat you
leaves you no choice
but to be reborn.

this is where i start again.
i pick myself up -
i don't worry about the tears.
they'll fall
but i'll ignore them.
i'll keep going -
try to smile,
make new friends,
write more,
travel the world,
hope i forget you,
hope you don't forget me.
hope that one day
i won't care quite as much
whether you do forget me
or not.
i'll admit to myself you were
just a person.
nothing more,
nothing that spectacular.
it'll be like it never happened
and eventually i'll feel the
air in my lungs again.

while you are
HEALING

while you are healing

i am painting over the walls,
i am ripping up the floor,
i am taking pictures out of frames,
putting new ones in.
i have rearranged the furniture,
repotted the plants,
and thrown out the trinkets
that have a little too much meaning.
i have changed the bed sheets.
i have changed the locks.
i have changed.
i am clearing you
from every inch of this space.
i am clearing you
from my heart.

you are more than the hurt.
you are more than people leaving.
you are more than tears.
you are more than heartache.
you are what comes
after all of that.

even on the days
the sky seems hollow
and i can't see the sun,
i know it's there.
i let this knowledge
bring me hope.

there are too many places
where you are wanted
for you to stay
where you are not.

i am relieved
that i grew tired
of begging for love.

i find myself
cheering when your team loses,
wishing for the rain i know you hate,
eating everything you thought was too spicy.
you left before i could say
fuck you.
so i've found another way.

every leaf
on every tree
is telling me that it's okay to fall.
this is not the end.

i can see who i might be
when i let you go.
she is beautiful and strong.
she is healed and her scars are scars
instead of fresh sores.
she sees the world in color,
not in black and white.
she knows she is worth something -
worth a lot,
worth everything.
she carries herself with grace
and she carries others too
(but this time, only the ones who deserve it)
she is no longer cowering,
disheartened,
empty.
she is everything i've ever wanted to be.
she is everything i couldn't be beside you.
she'll embrace me when i get there.
she will tell me it's okay.
she will forgive me.
she will love me.
she will know i did my best.
i'm not her *yet*,
but i am her.
and i know she is patiently
waiting for me.

is this how i ultimately
learn to love myself?
by defending myself
so vehemently
against your memory
that i start to see
there is truth in my defense -
i really do deserve better.

maybe every love is not
everlasting.
maybe some loves
lead you to other loves,
which lead you to others,
which lead you to yourself.

solitude won't break you.
fake love will -
don't settle.

holding on
and healing
are on different paths.
you must pick a direction.

parm k.c.

i saw you as a way
to escape myself.
i wasn't ready
for what a great love i could be.

i know i can do better
than accepting less than i deserve,
and giving more to others
than they deserve from me.

i know i can be better
than a girl who doesn't see her worth,
and a girl who feels she has no worth
unless others tell her she does.

i know i am better
than what i received,
and what i tolerated,
and what felt so wrong
but which i stayed in for far too long.

i can count the ways you hurt me
or i can count the opportunities
i have now that you are gone.
i choose the latter.

i do not sob every night
when the sun departs.
i know she is coming back.
i need a love that feels
just as sure.

in spring it rains
for days
and days at a time.
we don't question it.
we pull out the bins
that hold our raincoats and boots.
we splash in the puddles
and await the flowers.
we know better days are coming.
when you rain
for days
and days at a time,
remember this -
splash in the puddles.
await your flowers.

you might have taken a lot from me,
but you did not take me.
for better or worse
i am chained to myself.
this tether is the one thing saving me.

please strip off the hurt.
you do not need to wear it
like a coat of armor.
it is not a blanket
keeping you warm.
undress,
peel it off,
feel the air on your skin.
feel yourself return
to your natural state.
please strip off the hurt,
lay it down,
see how much lighter you feel.

the day you left,
i was mad at the sun
for shining.
how dare she feel so bright
when i did not.
now i know she was telling me -
take some of my light
until you can see your own again.

talk to nature,
tell it where it hurts.
tell the trees about your sorrow
and tell the river your story.
roll down a hill and notice how you
feel six years old again
while the heartbreak melts away.
blow fuzzy weeds into the wind
and see how they feel
free instead of uprooted.

i should not view the old me
with such disdain.
i am her,
reincarnated in this life.

you think you need a new set of arms
to fall into before you can move on.
so you wait,
stuck.
hoping for someone to save you.
but moving on doesn't need to involve
somebody else.
and your own arms should not be
overlooked.
it's possible to leave that space vacant
and still let go.

i have been wearing heartbreak
like a second skin.
but spring is coming
and the time for shedding is here.

this hurt is not forever -
nothing is.
one day you will sigh,
and let it go.

i hope to be good one day.
to feel the hole in my chest close up.
to feel more solid,
less unsteady.
to not buckle when i hear your name.
to see myself again
as something more
than yours.
i hope to be good one day.
and though i'm not yet,
this hope wasn't there before.
its presence tells me
there's a chance.

for so long,
i'd rather have swallowed the pain
than give it a voice.
i didn't want it to out me.
i didn't want it to tell the world
the story of how i'd let someone
hurt me,
suppress me,
turn me into nothing.
but eventually,
it bubbled up and made noise.
cried out.
told its side of the story.
it turned out pain didn't blame me -
it just wanted to be heard.

it is not your fault
they hurt you.
it is not your fault
you loved someone who hurt you.
you simply have healing to do.

somehow,
my voice is finding its way
out of the darkness,
into my throat,
and pouring out into the world.
it is quivering
but it's there.

there is not a shortage
of people who could love you.
let go of the one who doesn't.

it turned out the fear
of a life without you
was worse
than a life without you.
once you were gone,
i could exhale.

i can bury your memory,
or i can craft it into art.
either way it's nothing
but a memory,
and you no longer have
the power to hurt me.

no one good for you
will tell you to leave yourself.

alone
doesn't feel so lonely
after being with someone like you.

now i will lay you to rest.
i will hold a ceremony.
i will acknowledge the death
of what we had,
of what i pretended we had,
of your place in my life,
and of the me that existed with you.

stop looking
for someone to heal you.
start looking for healing itself.

grow.
not to teach them a lesson,
not to make them sorry,
not to bring them back.
grow -
so that you can move forward.

you are allowed to hurt.
you need not pretend you don't.
you are allowed to put your pain
under a microscope
and analyze it closely.
healing is not meant to be invisible.

maybe the silence
left behind in their wake
will allow you to finally hear yourself.

if you cannot take their words
and turn them into something
tangible -
something you can taste,
feel,
bathe in.
then their words are worthless.

i wondered why
you could not love me.
what could i be missing?
what fundamental flaw of mine
was so undesirable
that it prevented your love
from making its way into me?

so i didn't love me either.
i deferred to you
and thought you must be right.
but now that you've been gone,
and i've been in my own company -
loving me,
studying me,
and holding me,
i think -
maybe it's not that you could not love me.
maybe it's that you could not see me.

i am not made of paper.
i am not made of glass.
i am sturdier than this -
i am not so fragile
after all.

as much as i wish
i could forget you,
i wish i had the power
to make you forget me.
you don't deserve me
even in memories.

you know how you can overlook
all the flaws of someone you love
because you're hell-bent
on continuing to love them?
i'd like to tell you that you can do this
with yourself too.

be tender and forgiving
with yourself.
the days you feel lost
are the days you need
your own grace the most.

there is more to you
than this pain.
and there is more to your life
than the one who caused it.

i'm so sorry
that an imitation of love
made you feel like you don't deserve
the real thing.
you do.

don't let anyone tell you
they love you,
and then watch them
tear you down.
don't let anyone give love
such an awful name.

i cannot give anyone
all of my sun
or all of my rain.
i have my own soul to harvest.

your heart beats
even without him -
this living is for you.

when *alone*
is screaming too loudly,
instead of covering your ears,
ask yourself -
were you forsaken,
or were you set free?

i wish to be free.
i wish not to be shackled
by what you did to me.
i may always remember,
but i don't need to live in this prison
any longer.

the

joy

of

becoming

while you are healing

you tell me you miss me.
and for once,
instead of saying
i miss you too
i say,
i would too,
if i were you.
this is moving on.

i can no longer
cater to everyone
while starving myself.
i need to leave something
on my plate for me.

you introduced me
to the strongest version of myself.
i would not have met her
if you hadn't left.

you don't live in me.
you don't live in my head
and you don't live in my heart.
you were visiting for a while.
in fact,
i let you overstay.
but you don't live in me.
i am finally evicting you.

i always felt like something
was missing with us.
but i assumed something was
missing from me.
something i didn't have.
something i couldn't give.
something i couldn't be for you.
but then you left,
and whatever was missing -
this nameless, faceless thing
felt like it came back.
it turns out that when we were together
something wasn't missing from me after all.
something was taken from me.

falling in love with myself
feels so different
than it felt to fall in love with you.
with you it felt only like falling.
with me it feels like flying.

i once saw at the top of a mountain
a wildflower.
it was cold and barren,
and nothing else was growing up there.
but the wildflower
persisted.
every time i think i can't go on,
i remember.

other people don't get to decide
how much love you get,
how much you're worth,
what you deserve,
if you're beautiful,
or how much potential you hold.
you decide.
other people's thoughts on the matter
are nothing but noise.

the grief and the sadness
was your heart's way of saying,
you deserved so much more than that.

i don't hate her anymore -
the girl i was with you.
i don't think she meant to hurt me
or put me through that.
i think she just wanted love,
but didn't know what it should feel like.

leave the hurt
in the past.
commit to making
new memories.

i am not yours.
even if you love me,
even if i love you.
i am not yours.
i will always be mine.

i like myself more without you.
i like how i speak a little louder
and stand a little taller.
i like how my voice
doesn't tremble quite as much
and neither does my resolve.
i like how i get to watch the shows i like
and read the books that call to me.
how i get to make myself the main character
and feel at peace in my body.
i like how i see myself.
no longer through your eyes,
but through the eyes of someone
who loves me -
my own.

it gives me calm
to know that i'm not her anymore -
the one you wounded.
and to know that you
don't get to walk beside this healed me.

after you,
i think twice
before becoming a home for anyone else.
before letting them rearrange me
and remodel me
and suit me only to their needs.
after you,
i don't let myself
be a resting place for just anybody.
i am selective about the shelter i provide
and who i provide it to.
i cannot be four walls and a roof
to anyone who is merely a guest.

my body is my land.
you don't get to live here anymore.
you don't get to drain my resources
or my energy.
i am mountains and valley
and traversing me is not easy.
it's not for the faint of heart
and it's certainly not for those
who do not appreciate or respect me.
you don't own me just because you
think you found me.
you can't stay just because you
came upon my shores.
my body is my land
and i have the right to defend it.
against anyone who encroaches,
against danger,
against you.
my body is my land
and you don't get to use it anymore
as your safe space
or your soft place
to land.

and maybe now,
i will love myself.
for this is the one thing
i haven't tried yet.

-last resort

you did not make me.
you cannot take credit
for what i am today.
all the luminosity condensed within me
has nothing to do with you.
it showed its face when i healed from you,
but it did not come from you.
and there are plenty of cruel people
in this world -
i was bound to attach to one of them.
if it hadn't been you,
it would have been another.
i was, after all,
so blindly and so regrettably
unaware of my worth.
but i'm not anymore.
i see it now.
and i did that.
i got myself here.

time told me something
i will not forget:
that i was not crushed.
i was being shaped.

there's something about the way
i grow closer to myself
the further i go from you.
it feels like finding the home
i have been searching for all this time.

when he weaves himself
into your fragile skin,
then rips himself
right back out again,
it will hurt.
i promise,
it will hurt.
but when you take care
to sew your flesh back together
and patiently await the scars,
and then the healing,
the healing will come.
i promise,
the healing will come.

i asked the mountain
how to be so tall -
how to stand so proud.
it told me,
let your trials shape you.

you do not have to stay there -
in that place where you feel small.
in that place where you feel
like a fraction of what you really are.
you do not have to stay anywhere
you don't feel complete.

there will come a day
when you realize that darkness
has consumed you for too long.
and that pain has made a home
in a soul that is better suited for light.
this is the day that you will begin to heal.

you are not the sum of your heartbreaks.
when you add them up,
they will not equal your whole.
they are something that happened to you,
but they are not you.

you can fold yourself up
into halves,
quarters,
or more.
and still,
you won't be small enough
for the ones who feel
entitled to your space.
so fuck it.
unfold.

banish the belief that you aren't worthy.
it's not true.
it's not true.
it's not true.

-mantra

i feel like i'm
forgetting you.
it's the greatest gift
i've ever received.

we think that at some point
it will be too late to find love.
this couldn't be further from the truth.
look at how many people
in all stages and ages of life
are now discovering love
in themselves.

healing knew all along
that i was on my way to her.
i am so grateful that she waited for me.

time has dulled the edges
of these painful memories.
they no longer cut me.
they are just a reminder
of what i don't deserve.

there are so many reasons
why you may not have chosen me.
i see now,
none of them have anything
to do with my worth.
my worth is not measured
by who chooses me.

and just like that,
one night i went to sleep
missing you.
and woke up
without you on my mind.

i have stopped crying
over the girl i once was.
she was a stepping stone
to the woman i am now.

i am counting all of the things
i love about myself.
oddly enough,
the number matches evenly
with everything you criticized me for.
so i wonder now
if you honestly detested
those aspects of me,
or if you didn't want *me*
to see them clearly.
if you didn't want me
to see how much i didn't need you.

i am learning
that the parts of me i hide the most
are the ones i need to show the world
in order to heal.
and that if i open this vessel -
the one i have so desperately clamped shut -
something good might make its way in.

this is how i came to love myself:
i stopped believing the words
of those who do not love me.

they ask me how i healed,
and i tell them -
i grew tired.
of taking my pain
and shoving it into unseen corners.
burying it so deep
that not even an edge peeks out.
i grew tired
of covering it up with light,
so that no one would ever see
how black it was,
but saving none of that light for myself.
i finally let my pain be seen.

i am not responsible
for the way others love me
or don't.
i am responsible
for how i love others.
so if someone doesn't love me
in the way i deserve,
maybe that says more
about their propensity to love
and less about what i am worth.

i think you must have been holding
your hands over my eyes.
i only truly saw myself
after you were gone.

the more i tried to outrun the pain,
the more i felt like it was chasing me.
the moment i stopped,
turned around,
faced it -
pain stood still too.

there have been so many forms of me
that have lived in this body
and this mind of mine.
i am constantly meeting myself.
i need to say goodbye
to the one who hurt me
so the next version i meet is proud of me.

love will not ask you
to shrink yourself.
love will beg you
to grow.

i know now
i deserve a love that feels
like a deep inhale
after holding my breath
for far too long.
like air in my lungs
after years of choking
on whatever i was given
that seemed like love
but never really was.

be so close to yourself
that no one can ever come between
you and you.

healing feels like
so many things but
most of all healing feels like
finding peace with myself.

do not count the days
since they have been gone.
take that calendar off the wall -
do not weep at every anniversary.
the world is still spinning.
flowers are still blooming.
and so should you.

it turns out
it's easy to let people go.
you just need to hold on to yourself.

it is not enough to let go
of the people who hurt you.
you must also let go of the you
who thought you deserved that.

the thing about the love
you give yourself
is that it's not the type
that can be taken away.
when you do it right,
it's there when others love you,
and it's there when others don't.

one day you will see
that when they left,
they were wrong about you.

silence used to scare me.
it used to mean you were angry
or scheming
or a storm was brewing inside of you,
and it would make me
terrified.
i knew it meant
that something was coming
and it would not be anything
pretty.
but since you've been gone,
silence comforts me.
i can hear myself.
hear my thoughts,
hear the sounds
of the forest in my mind.
when it's silent now,
i don't have to fear i'm about to be broken.
i can sink into the quiet.
instead of breaking,
i can decide when i want to break
the silence.

i can't remember exactly when
i came upon myself.
i think it was somewhere
around the time
i left you behind.

care enough about yourself
to choose people
who care about you too.

your memory was a sliver
sitting beneath my flesh,
constantly throbbing.
painful,
but too much work to remove.
i couldn't bear to dig you out
so i let it sit,
living below the surface.
until it worked its way
up to the top,
close enough for me to pluck out,
examine,
and see that it was much smaller
than i'd ever thought.
i asked myself,
is this it?
is this the tiny thing
that has been causing all this hurt?

i'm with me for life
and i almost gave that up
many times
for someone who consistently
disregarded me.
i owe myself an apology.

i met her -
the woman that was underneath the weight
of you and your judgements
and everything you couldn't see.
she didn't trust me at first
because i'd stifled her for so long
and cloaked her behind
the opinions of others.
she didn't know how long she'd have
until i would tuck her away again
so she was timid
and quiet
and shy.
but i gave her time.
i coaxed her out.
i showed her that
everyone who'd stifled her is gone
and they won't be coming back.
i won't let them come back.
i promise i won't let them come back.

you're not a memory anymore,
you're an anecdote.
you could belong to anyone.
i've moved on, and you don't get to
be a part of me anymore.

falling out of love with you
was a revelation.
i realized there was
nothing magic about you -
i loved you
and that was your best trait.

i want to make my life
read like a love letter to myself.
i want to write it slowly,
gently,
in soft flowing cursive
that makes me smile.
i want to feel joy each time
i eagerly turn the pages
and read the words,
finding comfort in the way
it takes shape.
i want my life to feel
like a love letter -
you never wrote me one
and i see now that i never needed you to.

parm k.c.

for the first time
in a long time,
no one has a hold on my heart
except me.
i must admit it feels
so damn good.

it doesn't matter
how much you gave of yourself
to those who left.
you still have more
than enough for you.
you are so much love.

if i give you my heart
it is not because i trust you
not to break it.
it is because i have learned
i can restore it.
it is because i have learned
i am strong enough to heal again.

my mistake was feeling used
as though i am finite.
as though the forces of nature
won't return to me everything i am.
my mistake was not seeing
how immeasurable i am.

i thought if i cried enough,
you might come back.
i didn't expect that instead
i would wash away
every memory of you,
cry you out,
let you leave my system
through my tears,
feel empty for a bit,
and then be entirely replenished.

don't let anyone tell you
you love too deeply.
nobody tells the ocean
it contains too much life.

loving myself
feels like daybreak
after a long night of thinking
dark won't end.
loving myself
feels like receiving rain
when i was on the verge of wilting.
loving myself
feels like being brought back to life
just in time.

look how far i've come.
look at what i've built
out of the rubble you left behind.

there are some days
i remember you and it feels like
i am back there again.
scorned and breaking.
but then i look at myself and see
a smile on my face
that was absent for so long
and i remember -
i arrived at healing and you
cannot reach me here.

i am a different person
departing your heart
than i was when i entered it.
at first i didn't want to
get to know this me -
the one who walked out
looking nothing like the one
who walked in.
but now i think she is
who i was always meant to be.
she is why i met you.
i was never supposed to keep you -
i was always supposed to walk away
hand in hand with her instead.

little did i know
that you weren't permanent.
that you were only a season.
so when your leaves started falling
and you started leaving,
i didn't know what was happening.
i didn't know the cold that followed
was also just a season.
and that soon enough,
i would not remember the season of you
or the season after you.
that soon enough,
yet another season would arrive
and i'd have already forgotten you
and be basking in the sun.

i don't feel lonely anymore,
ever since i realized i have
more of me without you.

you didn't give me back all my things
and this used to make me sad.
you held on to my necklace and rings,
some t-shirts and a book.
i used to see these things
as not just things,
but as missed opportunities.
missed opportunities to have
seen you one last time.
missed opportunities to
change your mind.
missed opportunities
to pretend to get closure.
but now i've let some time slip by
and i don't see them
as missed opportunities anymore.
i don't see them
as things that i no longer have,
but as reminders to you
of what you no longer have.
and i realize i don't need those things back
anymore -
i'm doing just fine without them.
and i realize i don't need you back
anymore -
i'm doing just fine without you.

if i find love late,
it will not be late,
but right on time.
i will still have found love.
and love has no timeline,
no agenda,
no motive.
it doesn't need to get here fast.
it doesn't need to rush.
because when it's real,
it doesn't expire.
when it's real,
it waits for you.
it doesn't pressure you.
it doesn't tell you,
hurry up, or i'm leaving
without you.
it won't make you feel
like you can't take your time.
love will wait for me
just like i've waited for it.

i used to think i wanted someone
who would make me feel
like i was falling in love
all over again each day.
but why would i want to feel
like i am constantly falling?
why would i want to feel so unbalanced?
i want someone who lets me
lean on them,
hold on tight,
stay upright.
someone who loves me steady and
does not let me fall.

i have turned over every rock
and swam to the bottom of oceans
looking for what has always been
within me.

i should not have to tell you
to get off the ground -
he wasn't worth it.
he is not your God.
you should know not
to bow to him.
but if i have to tell you,
i'll tell you
so here it is -
get up and never
lower yourself for anyone
ever again.

there is comfort and relief
when a ship reaches the shore.
to know it was not lost at sea
is a victory of its own.
this is how it feels
to finally reach myself.

i am not looking for love.
i am too busy
being love.
if the one for me is ready,
healing,
looking.
they will find me.

eventually i will give
my heart to another.
i will fall headfirst
and let myself be
swept away.
i will convince myself
i've never felt this way before
and that this time -
this time
i have found the love of my life.
somehow,
the heart does find a way
to forget.

maybe everything
that you thought was breaking you
was actually leading you
towards yourself.

i cannot recall
the day i stopped missing you.
i'm not certain if it was a sunday
or a wednesday.
if it was raining,
or windy,
or warm.
i don't seem to remember
what i was wearing
or who i was with.
the details escape me,
as did the pain,
eventually.
the details don't matter.
what matters is that one way or another,
you stopped living in my mind that day.
i do know this for sure -
on that day i was released.

i am amazed at how the same bed
that felt too big after you left
now feels like freedom.
what once felt like loneliness
now feels like choosing my side,
having enough space,
sprawling out -
liberation.

if you unravel,
find the loose thread.
start there.
that's how you put yourself
together again.

there is peace
in my own embrace,
and i feel relieved
to have noticed it.
i feel like for once
i am giving myself a chance.

my life is my garden.
i cannot share my flowers with you
if you will not share your sunshine with me.

it was dark when you left,
but it did not stay dark forever.
i am so thankful
the light came home again.

i don't love you anymore.
i don't hate you anymore.
i don't think of you anymore -
i think this is healing.

i watch planes in the sky
and wonder where they're going.
how many people on them are hurting.
how many are lost.
how many have overcome something.
how many are still waiting to.
the planes seem so small in the sky -
like tiny tins full of hearts.
cutting through the clouds,
going from here to there.
i think about how we all
seem so small in the sky.
how we're all just trying to get somewhere.

i used to worry that i might just be a
collection of atoms of the ones who left. like
maybe there is nothing in me that is me. i
wondered if i am comprised only of their
remnants, woven together into a makeshift
quilt resembling something like the person i
see in my reflection. but the more time i
spend alone, i have come to the conclusion
that i am an amalgamation of all the me's i
was with those people. i am the
rehabilitation of each of those heartbreaks. i
am victories stacked up high, one on top of
another. i am edges of recovery sewn
together. and even though the job might not
have been done neatly - even though the
hem is not clean and you can see where the
ends were haphazardly stitched together - i
have been crafted into something beautiful.
i feel like a masterpiece.

now that you've been gone,
i've learned to come home to me.
this house doesn't feel so empty anymore.

i'm ready to stop writing about love.
more accurately,
i'm ready to stop writing about you.
i want to write about someone
new i have met.
and how i don't quite know her yet,
but i like her.
i can see myself loving her.
she greets me in the mirror
and she looks like the person
i've been searching for.
i want to write about how the mornings
feel different lately.
how i'm happy each time they arrive,
and how i don't feel so lonely
in my own head.
i want to write about what it feels like
to care about what happens to me
and where i end up.
i want to write about how i got here -
how i walked myself here
painstakingly,
dragging my feet,
falling frequently,
but arriving all the same.
and how i have no intention of ever leaving.

healing is here,
and i see now why i had to wait.
something this beautiful
was worth my patience.

i will describe it -
the way it feels to meet yourself.
it feels like removing splinters
of the ones who hurt you.
picking them out
from the depths of your skin
and from the corners of your brain.
it feels like outer layers unpeeled,
revealing raw *everything* underneath.
it stings briefly but adjusts in time.
it feels like removing the long day
from myself.
climbing under the covers
and waking up actually rested.
it feels like meeting the love of your life.

i wrote you down
and now i have no appetite
to read you.
the pages are bland -
my eyes gloss over them
while my mind roams and finds
stimulation elsewhere.
i recall reading you in
the same way i recall reading
something with pretty pictures
in the third grade that
i'm sure caught my interest
at the time.
but i'm older now.
not so much in age but in
experience and epiphanies
and i just don't have the desire
to read you when
there is so much of me and my story
to be writing.

some days,
it's the type of healing that
is quiet and brushes my cheek
softly.
some days,
it's the type of healing that
grabs me by the shoulders
the moment i wake,
shakes me,
and pulls me hungrily into the day.
every day,
i fall to my knees
and thank the universe
it's mine.

i'm so thankful it got too heavy
to carry around all the defeat.
to have a constant armful of heartbreak.
i am grateful for my wits end
for nudging me
towards a me who refuses
to continue like this.
trudging through heartbreak
like i can't move through it -
like i can't break away -
like it's quicksand
and i will only ever sink.
every day i wake up
and thank my heart for having a limit.

-gratitude

i thought it would hurt for an eternity -
i was certain of it.
but most things are not eternal.
i get to leave behind
the ones who have wronged me.
i get to choose what is everlasting -
what i carry and what i set down.
i get to look at time
and how it has both strengthened me
and put distance between me
and what broke me.
none of the hurt
that i thought would last for good
did.
i am so pleased
to have been so wrong.

i am tearing down
this barricade around my heart.
with bare bloody hands i am furiously
ripping,
grabbing,
pulling.
i am watching stones crumble.
i did not know destruction
could feel this beautiful.

at last, i am letting you
melt off my skin.
i am molting you
and making way for new
everything.
like a season shifting,
your leaves are separating
from my branches
and i do not
kiss them goodbye.
i am wringing the last drops
of you from me -
squeezing tight
until there is nothing left
but me.

if two years later,
or seven,
or ten,
you find the pain bubbling up,
and the memories feeling fresh
when you least expected it,
it won't mean that you are not healed.
it means trauma lives in the body
and we cannot simply erase the hurt.
it does not mean that you still love them.
but that the way they didn't love you
changed you.

i wish that i could talk to her -
the person i used to be.
i wish that i could sit her down
and tell her not to be so scared.
tell her that she won't
be heartbroken forever.
i want to cross time and space
to reassure her that she will heal.
she won't stay down.
she will feel whole again.
i wish i could carry
some of the burden for her.
i know how tired she is.
if only i could step back in time,
and make her hear me.
i know i can't.
so i'll wait here patiently.
knowing she'll catch up to me.
she'll see,
eventually.

i thought when i discovered myself
there would be noise -
that it would be loud and boisterous.
that i would be met with a parade
and streamers,
that there would be no missing it.
but it wasn't like that.
it was quiet and it was gentle.
it was a soft landing.
it was blink-and-you-might-miss-it.
it was, *where did she come from?*
it was a deep and steady exhale.
i wouldn't have it any other way.

if i am a book,
then you were a mere chapter.
i refuse to stop at you.
i refuse to stop reading.

one day,
you will be filled with as much love
as you poured into them.
and one day,
you will be filled with more.
i can't wait until you get there.

if you are wondering
how i let go of him,
i will tell you that i didn't.
instead,
i let go of the parts of me
that thought he was what i deserved.
i let go of the parts of me
that thought happiness couldn't be mine.
i let go of years of conditioning
and years of indoctrination
that told me i needed someone -
anyone at all,
regardless of whether they lift me up
or push me down.
i let go of a girl
who could not fathom her power,
her strength,
her gifts.
i let go of her,
and somehow he fell away too.

parm k.c.

i look at mountains
and i do not feel intimidated.
i look at mountains
and see myself in them.
weathered and shaped
by years of storms.
and only deserving of being approached
by the patient and the brave.

and if you search for me,
you will not find me
in the same place where
we said goodbye.
you will find me in the mountains,
praying to the sky,
thanking it for teaching me
how to rise above.

i finally let go of the rope
that had me bound to you.
i did fall,
like i was afraid i would.
but the landing didn't hurt
the way i thought it would.
i didn't break any bones.
there was no blood.
i am intact.
i am better than intact -
i am free.

after you,
i have changed.
i have discovered new songs.
new bands to call my favorite.
melodies that didn't even exist
when i was with you.
after you,
i have traveled to cities
that weren't on my radar
when we were together.
i have changed my hair and my look.
i have new clothes -
sweaters you have never touched
with buttons you have never undone.
i don't live in that tiny apartment anymore.
i am not surrounded by walls
that once contained your voice.
after you,
i have made new friends.
people who've only heard about
the damage you inflicted
instead of having been there for it.
i have transformed in every way
after you.
i am a completely different being
than the one you were with,
and i have learned that sometimes
letting people go
is letting yourself change.

i'm going to love me
like i used to love you.
wild and without limits.
fiercely and like my heart is on fire.

while you are healing

Parm K.C. is a Punjabi-Canadian writer
from Alberta, Canada. She is a mental health
advocate who has, from a young age,
harnessed the therapeutic power of writing
and poetry. She finds great fulfillment in
offering comfort and empathy to others
through her written words.

You can find her online and on social media
at @byparmkc.